D0522035

Dragon Days

stories & poems

illustrated by

BRETT BRECKON

PONT

For Mum and Dad in your golden year,
with love and thanks for everything.
B.B.

First Impression – 2004

ISBN 1 84323 301 0

© stories & poems: the authors
© illustrations: Brett Breckon

Designed by Olwen Fowler

This book is published with the financial support
of the Welsh Books Council.

Printed in Wales at
Gomer Press, Llandysul, Ceredigion

Contents

Introduction

Brett Breckon

You have to look hard – very hard – to see a dragon these days.

It wasn't always so, because dragons are of the earth, of the universe even.

You see, when the world was born, dragons emerged from the same spitting, fiery cauldron of pure new elements. And from the beginning, they were sensitive to things that affect the balance of the earth. And what do you suppose is the one thing that disturbs the rhythms of the earth and the seas, more than anything else? Mankind. The way human beings behave on this planet.

So it's no surprise that dragons have always taken pains to avoid contact with people. Above all things, it is peace and quiet that dragons cherish most.

To people, dragons have often seemed terrifying. Their size, their shape and their ferocious appearance frightened many people, and, yes, some dragons can breathe fire! So, in people's minds, dragons became demons.

Cavemen hunted them, even though they couldn't eat them. Later, knights sought honour by questing against them. Sometimes, they would hunt a dragon for decades, imagining that they were ridding the world of a demon, but all the while the dragon would really be looking for peace and quiet. Staying ahead of a clumsy, noisy, smelly knight was pretty easy to a dragon with his sensitivities. But sometimes it would get so bad that the dragon would just have to eat the knight, to end the hassle.

Every now and then a knight would get lucky and kill a dragon, and cut off its head. Or, if the dragon was too

4

big, the knight might pull out a dragon tooth as a trophy . . . before the poor dragon turned to dust and returned to the earth. You won't find dragon bones or fossils.

All of this drove dragons to the quietest corners of the world. The Celtic races seemed more in tune with them than other peoples, and for some time Wales, Ireland and Scotland became safe havens for dragon families. It was probably just a short time, about 500 years maybe, but it was a good time. Though the dragons were almost never seen, they were there.

Eventually the peace was broken. By industry, machines, factories, pollution. A lot of people came to the wild, ripping at the earth for its treasures. Dragons had to retreat again.

From the wild shores, the highest mountains, the deepest caves, and from the sea, the dragons watched from afar as hamlets grew into villages, then towns, then cities. Men created machines of every kind, and then the machines flew. The air became dirty. There was more noise. And now, in the wars between people, men used their newest, fastest machines.

So, in the twentieth century many dragons left the Celtic lands. But not all. There are rugged coasts, dark caves and mountain peaks which people have not yet spoiled. Those are the places, often the westernmost places, where you may still see a dragon.

I love to explore the coast in my kayak, finding hidden coves, spotting secret caves, and studying the wild, rugged clifftops. They often seem so deserted - but are they? Can I always be sure that what I see is cliff-face, seaweed or rockpool? There is a feeling of timeless, secret mystery out there, and from that sprang the dragons in this book. My family wonders where I had the ideas for them... I'm not sure I really know.

I'm sure of one thing, though: you will never see a dragon from a 4x4 or a jetski, for they'll see, hear, feel and smell you a long way off. But you might chance upon one if you are quiet, unassuming and have good intentions. And if you do and you look into his eyes, you will see centuries of calm wisdom staring right back at you.

So if you look hard, very hard, you may still see a dragon, even these days.

5

$\mathcal{I}$n the Beginning

Gillian Clarke

omebeing sat in the dark, thinking. The dark place was Nowhere. It was no-time.

Nobody – not you, not I – knows what Nowhere was like, or what Somebeing looked like. There were no eyes to see, no ears to hear. There were no words, no names, no things. The story was at its very beginning, and there was nobody to remember or to tell it.

Somebeing was not a He or a She. Somebeing was It. It sat in the dark, thinking. We know Somebeing must have been thinking because of what happened next. Thinking can cause trouble. Thinking leads to ideas, and ideas make us restless. We can't keep still. We fidget and fuss. We rummage and pester for bits and pieces to make our idea real.

The first idea ticked in the dark inside Somebeing. It would be the most brilliant idea in the history of the Universe. It hummed and grew and brewed and swelled like a thunder cloud. It could not be stopped. At last it burst and ripped through the darkness faster than light, faster than sound – though light and sound had not yet been born.

In no-time there is no past, no present, no future. The first idea had no beginning and no end, no head, no tail. Once it was free it snaked out through

6

the dark, sinuous, serpentine, unstoppable. It set off through Nowhere, not from here to there, because here and there did not exist. Not from now to then, because Time had not begun. It went and came all at once. On the way out on the road to Nowhere, it met itself coming back. The collision created one almighty bang, the biggest bang that would ever happen. It was the mother of all explosions, and out of it the Universe was born.

How long did it take in Earth-time for the Big Bang to turn nothing into something? How long for the dust, the smoke and the gas, the cinders and the sparks to die away, leaving a bright new Universe behind? How long for a Universe to be born? Four and a half billion years is so much time it makes your head spin, like thinking of forever and ever.

The echoes of the Big Bang rippled out, out, out into Nowhere. The echoes are rippling still, farther and farther into outer space to this very day. Then a great wind rose and fell. The dust slowly settled. The fires died down leaving stillness and silence.

At first the sky seemed empty. Then, one by one the stars came out, as they do at nightfall in our world. They twinkled over a small, stony planet bowling along inside a new galaxy in the new-born Universe, a planet with an iron heart, a planet still hot and molten. The planet towed a little moon behind it, like a cow leading its calf. It rolled as it travelled along the space-road in the track of its fellow planets. Then, suddenly, as it turned over in the dark, the miracle happened, the miracle that would make it special. Close by was a huge star. It was just close enough for the planet to wake in the brightness and warmth of the very first morning of the world. Planet Earth glowed in the Sun's fire.

Earth. Air. Fire. Water. These things, and the soup of chemicals left by the Big Bang in the great laboratory of the galaxy, were just what was needed to make Life begin. But not yet. This is just the beginning of the story.

Inside the starry spiral of the Milky Way, the restless Earth turned as it travelled on its path round the Sun, its moon trailing like a little boat behind a ship. The Sun warmed first one side of the Earth, then the other, tickling the chemicals, making things fizz and ferment, making thunder and lightning, earthquakes and tornadoes. The oceans swayed to and fro as the moon pulled

8

them and let them go. The mountains rumbled. They spat, fizzed and farted. They hummed and burped. Earth's skin shivered as if it were shaking off a fly. It quaked, cracked and crackled. Its plates of rocky armour creased and crumpled as they closed again. There was never a quiet moment.

And in Somebeing's imagination, something was cooking. What would be the first living thing to be born on Earth? Would it be it a germ? Would it be a virus? A wriggle in a warm swamp? Long before the slow, slow work of making Life had even begun, the idea for the first creature was incubating. It was to be Somebeing's wonder. It was to be the world's storyteller.

One very small flame came flickering out of the nine-hundred-and-ninety-ninth exploding volcano. It licked its way over the lava, picking up metals and minerals as it went, burning sometimes blue, sometimes green, sometimes red. At first it was frail and naked as a fledgling, small and tender, a waif lost in the storms of a shifting Earth. But as it touched the new rocks of the Earth, as it licked the salts and the irons, it was transformed. It grew stronger and braver, bigger and faster as it went.

Many dangers lay ahead. When the Flame reached the edge of the ocean, a great wave reared its head and rolled out of the sea to crash onto the shore. The Flame felt a swipe of salt water. It hissed and faltered, gulping for air – fire needs air to survive. It almost drowned. Then, at the last moment, as the wave fell back into the sea, the Flame flickered and burned up again more strongly than before. It sizzled over the molten lava bubbling at the foot of a volcano. A cloud of ashes lifted from the lava-flow, and fell onto the flame. Almost suffocated, it fell back as if it were dead. Then a rush of wind lifted the ash and swirled it away. The Flame burned up bravely and licked its way over the lava where old fires were still smoking. The rush of wind which had saved it picked up speed and power, and blew the Flame until it all but died. If it died now, forgotten before it began, it would be forgotten forever. The world's story was only just beginning. Without a storyteller, who would hear it? Who would remember? Only a mythical creature born in the first imagination, always ready with its tongue of fire, could whisper our story into our minds. Like a secret passed from speaker to listener, parent to child, our story would live forever and ever.

We will call the Flame, Vulcana, daughter of the volcano, child of fire. Vulcana survived her great adventure. She grew wings from the clouds of the air. She grew a tongue and a tail from forks of lightning. Her skin was scaly like the plates of the Earth. Her breath was the wind. Her feet uncurled like buds in spring, but tough as the iron heart of the Earth. Her toes were diamonds and emeralds. She could tread on boiling lava. She could walk in your dreams four-thousand-million years before you were born.

Having set the Earth going in its lovely Universe, Somebeing had nothing else to do but sit back and hope for the best. The stars were in their places. The planets were on track. Earth was the perfect planet, the one singled out for special favour. Chemicals were at work on land and sea, seething and simmering in the light and heat of the sun. Evolution was at hand to move things along. All Somebeing could do now was just be. A cloud, a shadow, a rainbow. Perhaps a summer afternoon, or a thunderstorm, or one of those skies

that make you say, 'Looks like rain!' Anything to suit the mood of the moment while passing the time dreaming up creatures of the future. With any luck, one fine morning in a few billion years, a huge boulder might turn its head and wink, and Somebeing might think, 'That's it! Another brainwave! Dinosaurs!'

A few billion years. That was a long time . . .

Time! Already, Somebeing could see that Time was a bad idea. In fact, it would be a terrible nuisance, and there was going to be an awful lot of it. The trouble was, once Time was out of its box, nothing could stop it. Whether it crept, or whether it flew, nothing could be done to control it. One day it would make people say things like, 'You're late!', and 'Oh! No! Is that the time?' and 'Are we nearly there?' It would make birthdays go too fast, and getting old come too soon. In the end there would be machines to measure it, and special police to make sure you use your time well, and never, never waste it. Too late now. The deed was done and Somebeing knew it.

Meanwhile, Vulcana crawled into a cave and fell asleep. She, born from a volcano, the future mother of all dragons, mother of all stories, lay as still as a lizard in her rocky ravine. A she-dragon is a patient creature. There she would wait for three thousand five hundred million years for Life to begin, and a thousand million more for the first human being to be born.

She would wake only when the first person on Earth imagined her, and named her. Then she would begin to whisper the world's stories into human ears. She would lay her dragon eggs in caves and crevices. When her young hatched, they would travel on the backs of thunderstorms to every land on Earth. Her offspring would have many names. Soon there would be dragons everywhere, in every land, in every century, asleep until a human story woke them. Then, at two shakes of a forked tail, they would stir from their long hibernation and begin. At the beginning.

Dream-catching Dragons

Julie Rainsbury

High on a rooftop, a weathervane spins
and its silhouette dragon stretches her wings,
they beat in the sunshine, splinter the light,
spread wide to lift her into magical flight.

This is the dream of a boy in the street
waiting for the school bus, bag at his feet,
he thinks of her gliding, zooming so fast –
looses his golden dragon – imagines the first.....

● ● ● ● ●

Once upon a time, in the then before now,
when the world was still new and people unfound,
sudden as a shaft of sunlight through cloud,
a great golden dragon spun towards the ground.
She swooped over plains and unfurling trees,
skimmed newly-cracked cliff tops, crossed bubbling seas,
ringed the movement of mountains like a halo, a glory,
blazed a trail through that time before words, before history.
The rhythm of her wings as she circled earth's bounds
made whole galaxies thrum with tumultuous sound.
Her body seemed molten, her crest was so bright
it flickered and shimmered – banishing the night.

12

She polished the moon, until it mirrored her scales,
with a huff of her fire-breath, a swish of her tail,
banked steeply and soared through as yet unnamed stars,
licked each one with flame so they glowed from afar.
Her talons were luminous, her smile fanged with sparks
as she ripped through the sky and slashed through the dark.
She could slither, so sinuous in her silk-subtle sheen
then flash, as she turned, to a honed-metal gleam.
A tongue sharp as lemons yet honeyed with song,
limbs gorgeous with gold dust, incredibly strong,
eyes craters of lava, brazen ambers that swirled
in a glister of glistening as she twisted and twirled.
She was sunburst so yellow, a beacon of light,
a fireball, a comet, such a wondrous sight,
she was glitz, she was glamour beyond any dream
yet tears poured her path like a gilded slip-stream.
Across heavens, empty lands, an ocean's cold foam,
always solitary, so lonely, friendless she roamed.

● ● ● ● ●

A brush rinsed in water – and ultramarine
seeps a shape-shifting stain, some mysterious djinn
that forms a sea-dragon before you can blink,
slips from the jam jar to escape down the sink.

He wriggles, floats, dives, tumble-turns his way
through drains, streams, rivers – fins out to the bay.
This is the dream of a schoolgirl in class –
she launches a blue dragon – imagines the first…

● ● ● ● ●

Long, long ago before time had a measure,
when all things were young, in the old never-never,
at the deepest dark fathom of the darkest deep sea,

13

far from all brightness, the breath of winds blowing free,

far from that lullaby of waves finding shore,

far below storm currents, on ocean's fogged floor,

a shadow like a breaker wavered, sea-changed,

flooded indigo as squid-ink then ebbed back again.

Eerie, translucent, it rippled and reared

to a sea-monster, a dragon with a waterfall beard.

His blues were the blues of all the earth's oceans

and whirl-pooled his body like a sea-wizard's potion.

As he swam gulfs and channels, buoyed on the swell,

his wake was awash with starfish and shell

which echoed his passage with their sea-muted chime

all tangled in the weeds that streamered his spine.

Web-footed and fingered with narwhal-horn nails,

rudder-tailed, gill-eared, wings wide as full sail,

he slicked straits of icebergs, surged his way south

to lagoons that were languid, tepid as a bath.

He butterfly- and breast-stroked, floated on his back,

crawled barnacle-encrusted and dripping sea-wrack.

He explored every bay, each inlet and cove,

dived uncharted sea-caves searching for love.

His sorrow was awful, he cried and he keened,

wept wild tears of sapphire and aquamarine.

He writhed and he thrashed a tidal wave so high

that, when he surfed on its crest, his scales scraped the sky.

Then a rush towards the shore, a crashing of billows,

the sea's shushed retreat, the dragon beached in the shallows.

● ● ● ● ●

A circle of hills surrounds the town

like two curled-up dragons asleep on the ground.

Wind stirs the ridge of each rocky spine,

whistles through hollows till they both breathe in time.

14

Quickened by cloud-race, flanks uncoil as the pair
unleash turf-tethered limbs, awake in their lair.
This dreamed by children at play on the grass –
they rouse two green dragons – imagine the first…

• • • • •

In mists beyond memory, those most ancient of days
when earth sang so dew-fresh and people held no sway,
the great, golden dragon searched for the source
of a dreadful lament that grew steadily worse.
She found the blue dragon quite breathless and battered
weeping pools among the rocks, all tide-ripped and tattered.
She coaxed and she tended, she nuzzled a smile,
stroked his tempest-torn scales so that, in a short while,
they paddled together – now no longer alone –
let the sea lap his wounds until all pain was gone.
Then they danced, they pranced, they swam round and round,
leapt over the waves, roared their laughter out loud,
they tossed the spray high, they plashed and they plunged,

15

splashing each other as they frolicked and lunged.

Her sun-gold on his back. His sea-blue on her skin.

Their colours mixed together – until both were green.

They were washed in sleek emerald, all sad times gone by

just recalled in their blue flecks, the gold of their eyes.

Then they barrel-rolled planets, carouselled each pole,

linked their tails as they plummeted into free fall.

They swished across forests, swooshed the tall grass,

sputtered fireworks of joy towards the future, the past.

For the present they settled – dragon queen, dragon king –

bedded into the earth and entwined like a ring.

● ● ● ● ●

Dragons from antiquity or newly glimpsed today

Dragons fond of peace and quiet, whatever others say

Dragons sculpted out of stone, dragons cut from paper

Dragons who go by other names: worm, wyvern, *y wiber*

Dragons drawn in margins on some ancient maps

Dragons raised as figureheads or sewn on baseball caps

Dragons gaped as gargoyles, dragons flown as kites

Dragons pestered by maidens and harried by fierce knights

Dragons atop a gatepost, a guildhall or a fountain

Dragons tiny as a flea, gigantic as a mountain

Dragons who nibble broccoli and feast on cabbage leaves

Dragons with lairs underground, those who nest in trees

Dragons cute and cuddly, fluffy as a toy

Dragons bold with daring-do, but mostly shy and coy

Dragons flying on a flag or painted on a bus

Dragons trying hard to live side-by-side with us

Dragons gathered together: a flock, a shoal, a herd?

Dragons that are down-to-earth or quite out-of-this-world

Dragons numbered in your mind instead of counting sheep

Dragon stories dream-captured when you're fast asleep...

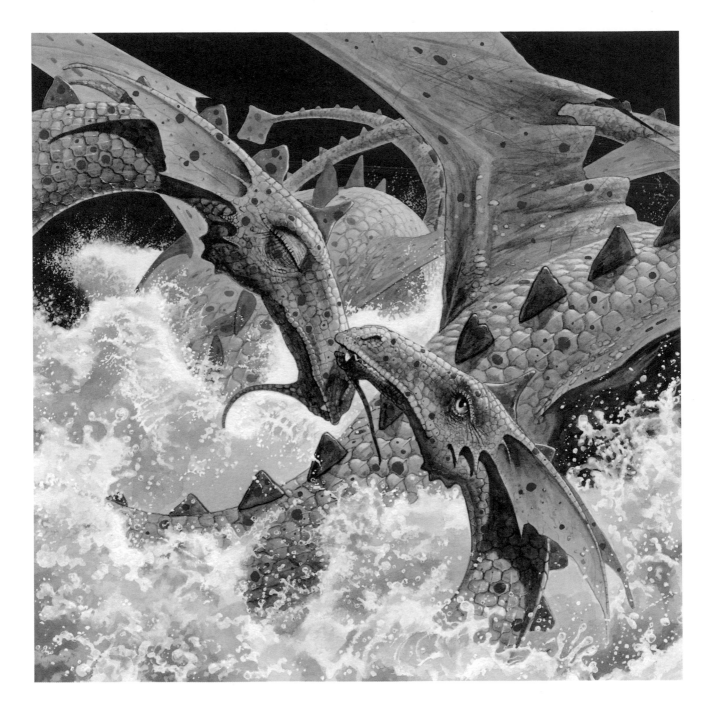

Dragon Pale

Mary Medlicott

Dragon Pale came into a world of shadows. Vicious swooping shadows were cast by flying monsters that brought terror to young and old alike. Dark-winged ones would dive down from the sky, seize dragon babies in their beaks or claws and carry them away. The older dragons were deeply distressed. They possessed no language, had no words to describe things or name them. Yet these ancient and magic beings had instincts and feelings just like us. More! They were peace-loving creatures, and despite their great strength and size, they had no heart to fight the monsters that darkened their skies.

Like other young dragons, Dragon Pale had milky-white skin and a gentle, patient expression. Whether she would survive to adulthood was, however, uncertain. The dragons in the West were on the run. They hid out of sight in caves with their young, allowing them outside to frolic only at dawn or dusk when they might not be seen.

Not until the monsters began raiding the dragons' caves did the dragons finally rise against them. As baby after dragon baby was targeted and clawed away, the adult dragons gathered. They had no word for it, but this was war.

There were endless days of attack and retreat, of charging and fleeing, until at last there was a mighty battle. Earth shook beneath the force of the bodies that came falling out of the air, locked in mortal combat. The air

18

filled with terrible shrieks. Deep in their caves, young dragons quailed as the sounds of warfare reached even there.

Silence finally arrived but no dragon parents returned. The young ones began to whimper, crying in hunger and fear. Hours went by, until Dragon Pale finally knew she must find out what had happened. As the oldest of the dragon young, she had been left to look after the babies. Now she could bear it no longer. Uncoiling her long, pale body, and ignoring the younger dragons' cries, she lowered herself into the ink-dark water and swam through the channel that led to the sea. It was dawn when she emerged. A huge blood-red sun was rising. Seeing it, Dragon Pale shivered. Except for the gentle lapping of waves, everything around her was deathly still.

Dragon Pale looked up. She saw no swooping shadows. Scanning the rocky coast with her big, dark eyes, she saw no monsters there either. Nor could she see a single dragon. She turned for the nearby sandy beach and began to swim in on the tide. Like a surfer waiting for the strongest wave, she coiled and uncoiled her body until, finding her wave, she began moving her wings. Three wing-flaps later, she rose into the sky.

Dragon Pale flew straight for the mountain that marked the northern boundary of her home. She couldn't have said why she went that way. She just knew she had to go there. As she approached, she saw what she feared. On the grassy-green slopes of the mountain, masses of bodies littered the ground. The sight froze Dragon Pale's blood. Huge purple-black bodies of dark-winged monsters lay interpersed with those of the last, brave dragons. She circled lower and wider, searching the scene of devastation.

When Dragon Pale saw her own dragon family, her parents and brothers and sisters and cousins, lying on the bright green grass, their bodies gashed and broken, she could hardly bear to continue. She flew lower, and saw with increasing dread that they were all losing their colour. Each second that passed, her beloved family became paler as the green of their bodies seeped away. Dragon Pale was sick at heart. She landed softly beside the outstretched bodies of her dragon father and mother. Sadly, gently, she reached out towards them. Tears welled in her dragon eyes until something made her stop and listen. Soft sounds like singing were coming from her

19

dragon parents – as if they were alive and knew she had come. Soon the whole tribe of dragons was singing! She realised then that none was dead.

What was it, then, that made Dragon Pale leave, flying immediately back to the coast? Already she knew that in their battle against evil monsters, the dragons must have possessed some source of power that still lived, that refused to be stamped out. If they were truly to survive, she was the only one who could help.

Dragon Pale flew straight for the open ocean towards the place beyond the headland where the currents met and the waters swirled. She had been there before with other young dragons but never been allowed to linger. Always, adult dragons had nudged them away as if it was a place of danger. Now Dragon Pale had no hesitation. As she came over the swirling blue waters, she first raised her head towards the sky; then swiftly folding her pale-white wings, she drew her limbs into her pale-white body and, dipping seawards again, arrowed herself into the water.

The ocean was deeper than she could have imagined. Yet Dragon Pale swam for the bottom. She could not have known why, she just knew she had to do it. As she sank deeper and deeper, the young dragon felt the weight of the water above her and fear at what might lurk below. When she saw the flash of fishes, noticed the sparkle of shells, she knew she was nearing the seabed. But as her clawed feet found soft sand at the bottom, she saw that she was looking at a different world. Ahead were rocks and a kind of huge open cave, its entrance a shell-studded archway. Fronds of coloured weed waved across it like curtains. Brown seaweed reached back into the waters beyond. Drawn towards it, Dragon Pale folded her wings against her body and pushed through the fronds. On the seabed beyond lay an island of green.

Dragon Pale moved forward. She knew at once that this was what she had come for. Yet once again, she knew she had to leave swiftly. But how? As she turned to go back through the archway, she could no longer see it. Fronds of red and brown seaweed overwhelmed her, completely blinding her vision. She stumbled forward to find herself bumping blindly against rough rocks. The sharp tips of shells bruised her head and her body as, again and again, she pushed against the tangle of seaweed, trying to get free of it.

But the harder she pushed to get free, the more she sensed this underwater world binding itself to her body. Brown seaweed was lacing itself round her neck and shoulders, making bold patterns on her milky-pale skin. Red and striped fronds of seaweed were attaching themselves to her face, adorning her eyes and her mouth. Blue shells were fixing themselves along the length of her neck. Dragon Pale felt as if an enormous weight was fastening itself to her. For a moment, it felt impossibly heavy; she wanted to stop and give up. But with one more heave, she found the archway and was through it and swimming up to the ocean's surface.

She could not have told how long it took her to get back. She just knew that the weight behind her was too heavy for her to be able to fly. She had to swim, pulling whatever it was behind her. When she finally reached the shallows, she was almost too exhausted to look back to see what it was that had been pulling at her. When she did, she saw, just below the sea's surface, a wide green meadow, its grasses waving with the movements of the water. As the meadow surfaced, blades of fresh green grass began poking through the reflections and emerged, glistening. A mound, a slope, a bank and a curve of shore all rose up out of the water. From the depths of the ocean, Dragon Pale had brought home a magic island.

Dragon Pale fell back exhausted until, suddenly, the sounds of dragons reached her from the shore. She knew those voices. The young ones must have come out from their caves and discovered their wounded dragon elders. Amongst the shrill calls of the baby dragons, however, Dragon Pale then also heard the deeper calls of adults. Lifting herself to her feet, she turned to see that her whole dragon tribe was coming towards her from the slopes where so many had fallen. As pale as their young ones now or paler, the adult dragons were being led by the young ones. Her eyes wide with amazement, Dragon Pale scanned the mass of painfully lumbering figures and with delight observed that none of the dragons was missing. All her loved ones were coming towards her.

Slowly the wounded dragons came to the place where Dragon Pale stood, her long pale neck now beautifully marked with brown patterns and studded with unusual blue shells, red and striped fronds adorning her face like ribbons. With each minute that passed, the adult dragons seemed to be gaining in strength. Each one embraced her, then surged past and onto the island's green surface. There they soon began rising in a joyful dragon dance. Their bodies coiled and uncoiled, their great wings beat out a rhythm, as strength and colour flowed back into their veins. What Dragon Pale had brought them was a magic green island, one of the magic floating islands that still occasionally rise to the surface in the seas of West Wales today.

But for now, the dragons did not think of the future. They rarely do. At this particular moment in their history, they were full of joy. Dragon Pale had brought them what they needed: a place of healing and refreshment. Now there would be peace for their bodies to be mended and their spirits refreshed; peace to see them through into the unending future – where one day there would be a language in which to tell their stories.

● ● ●

23

Cerrig and the Bridge of Ice

Michael Ponsford

Cerrig waits at the sea's edge, snakes her neck, breathes heat, gasping. But not fire, not again. Cerrig remembers.

She came from another place. She remembers that there were green mountains split by wild white rivers, and there were cliffs and crags, and often a strong wind blowing through the valleys. She had lived there with her mother and father, the youngest daughter in a family of blue-gold scaled dragons.

These are the sort of dragons who are able to fly in childhood; but as they grow older and their snaky necks lengthen, and the armour of scales becomes heavier, their wings will no longer lift them; then they are called grown-dragons, and must leave their families. Cerrig could not remember her sister and brothers, who had become grown-dragons and left when she was very young.

But Cerrig remembers well the day when she left the wild place in the mountains to travel to the Great Meeting of New Grown-Dragons. Her mother and father were sad that she had to leave, but proud that she could now learn the wisdom of all dragons, and then leave for a new place where she would become the mother of her own dragon family.

Nobody told Cerrig the way to the Great Meeting.

'Just follow the path that you think is right,' her father had told her, 'and it will be the way. It will take the passing of three moons, but you will find the place.'

So Cerrig had set off down the track beside the tumbling white river, until she came to a wide valley where the river flowed smoothly, and there was a sacred stone which told Cerrig without words that she was on the right path. She travelled over high hills that unfolded for days in front of her, mist-laden and cool; she made her way through wild-woods, haunted

24

by the ghostly sound of owls, who have their own wisdom; she climbed through stone-struck dry valleys, where the dust blew spitefully in her eyes. She slept when darkness fell, but with one eye open, watching the moon as it changed its shape night by night.

Her father was right. After the passing of three moons, she reached a wide plain in the hollow of the hills, with a circle of stones in its grassy centre. They were put there, she was told, thousands of years before, by the gods of the dragons. And there were new grown-dragons of all sorts arriving at the same time as Cerrig: massive red-burnished dragons with great billowing wings; tiny green dragons that scurried over the stones, hissing and spitting; and some like herself, with blue-gold scales and heavy, snaky necks. The wide field was seething with dragons.

Then a dragon-voice roared, and all the dragons were still. Cerrig cowered with fear.

'I am the Wise-Mother of the Dragon Clans,' said the voice, the noise echoing around the hills, and Cerrig saw that it came from a huge, ghostly-pale dragon in the middle of the plain. The voice roared again. 'We have gathered here today to share the wisdom of Dragons, so that you, the new-grown of your clans, may take this wisdom to the four corners of the world, and keep the Dragon-lore alive, as it has been alive for thousands of years.'

Cerrig listened in wonder, and all the other dragons listened too. For a seven-night they listened as the Wise-Mother of the Dragon Clans spoke, her voice soft now, telling them of the wisdom that they should hold in their hearts. She told them about the lines of power that thread the world, scorched there by the fire of dragon-gods at the beginning of time, so that all dragons could find their true journey. She described how the dragon-gods created the seasons, and tamed the tides to follow the pull of the moon. She explained about clouds, which are no more than the breath of dragons; and thunder, which is their anger. Finally, they were told about fear.

'There is a new race,' said the voice of the Wise-Mother, as darkness fell on the seventh night, 'a new race who cannot yet know the secrets of the world, and for this we must fear them. This race of creatures, who call themselves men, have brought fear of all things into the world, and because

26

they fear, they also hate. So we must fear these men.'

The next morning, the dragons departed from the Great Meeting, each of them seeming to know which way their journey should take them. Cerrig knew that she must go to another land that lay across the sea, and as she set off over the hills, she found another dragon on the same path, and knew that he would journey with her. His name was Tegid, and he had come from his home near a lake, high in the hills.

'We will find a forest of twisted, ancient oaks,' he said to Cerrig.

'And it will take us more than one moon to pass through the forest,' she replied, 'and then we must wait at the sea's edge.'

'At the sea's edge,' Tegid continued, as if their voices were the same, 'until winter comes, and the drifting ice-islands will build a causeway across the sea to the new land.'

So it was as if they had always known each other, and their journey. Cerrig was happy to be travelling with Tegid.

The journey took a long time, longer than the three moons it had taken to reach the Great Meeting, but Cerrig did not notice how hard their travelling was, or how far she had journeyed. At last, they came to a huge forest of twisted oak trees. It was spring-time, and the leaves of the trees were pale green and shimmered with light, and there were white flowers, bright in the sunlight that fell through the branches, and birdsong. Cerrig did not believe that she had ever been so happy, and this was their home until winter came. She and Tegid made their way slowly through the forest, talked to each other of their families, of the wisdom that they had learned, and of the future.

Spring passed into summer, and shadows darkened under the oaks where they slept at night. Then came days when the sun was lower in the sky, and not as fierce, and the leaves burned gold on the branches, then fell in thick drifts on the forest floor. Cerrig and Tegid made their way to the edge of the forest, where the sea roared and tumbled on a beach where the last of the oak trees grew, and waited. They saw ice-islands, green as their own eyes, drifting on the sea, and felt the cold harden in their scales. A bitter wind blew, flecked with snow. They found a cave hidden amongst the forest rocks to hide in from the cold. Still they waited, listening to the wind in the trees, the crashing of the waves.

27

But one morning, when snow had muffled the forest, Cerrig heard a different sound, and it chilled her with a fear stronger than the cold wind. It was a hollow, thudding noise, with a dead, repeated rhythm. Tegid heard it too, and Cerrig saw the same fear in his eyes. In the bay, the ice-islands were drifting together, the rough wind and the tides building them into a bridge that would let the dragons finish their journey. But the bridge was not yet ready.

The rhythmic thudding came again, and then again, and Cerrig's heart turned with fear. She prayed for the ice-bridge to be complete that day.

The next day the thudding noise was nearer, and more fearful. And then there was a fierce roaring sound, like the river Cerrig had once lived beside. But this roaring was full of pain; then there was a sound of breaking branches, and of thunder, an explosion of noise. Birds scattered. Cerrig saw light burst into the forest. A huge oak tree lay on its side. And in the clearing next to it, a group of men, with their wild hair and their hard eyes, holding axes.

'We must hide,' said Tegid. But the men were already pointing and shouting, and then more came out of the forest, hundreds of them, with their spears and knives, their blades and their cries of hatred, and they ran at the two dragons. Cerrig took off through the trees. She crashed blindly in the forest snow, spinning amongst the bare oaks, hearing the voices of the men behind her. She looked back, and saw Tegid moving too, but towards the beach.

'Ice-bridge,' he called to her above the noise of the men. 'Ice-bridge, Cerrig. It's ready.'

Cerrig turned towards him, and saw him reach the edge of the forest, flailing across the snow-freaked sand of the narrow beach. But here the men could throw their spears and their blades, and they clattered madly on Tegid's scales. Cerrig knew that just one spear that found the flesh under the blue-gold scales or his frightened eyes could bring him down.

'Ice-bridge,' he called again. Cerrig saw that he was almost there: the wind had pushed the last of the ice-islands into place, just as they had known it would, and there was their road to another land. She crashed through the trees towards him, the soft sand of the beach beneath her, her breath roaring.

But there were men there too. They raised their spears.

Cerrig breathed her fear, roared her breath-burst towards them. And her

28

breath was full of fire. She turned back into the forest, blind again with fright, and roared again, turning her head. Fire leapt across the snow. Beyond the trees, she saw Tegid on the ice-bridge. Safe. She roared more flames. She crashed amongst the trees. She fled. At last she reached their hidden cave. The men had lost her. She watched them walk back towards the shore, heard the hatred in their voices.

But they were not finished yet. Cerrig saw one man lift a branch of wood from the forest floor where she had breathed. It smouldered still. The man cupped his hands, and blew on it. Smoke thickened in the air. The branch crackled. And then the men were busy with more wood. Cerrig retreated into the cave, and listened to the laughter, smelt the smoke of bigger fires.

The men left the forest, and Cerrig waited. The fires burned for days, and still she waited. She watched the passing of a moon and more, and still the fires choked the air with acrid smoke, roared through the forest of twisted oaks. The sun grew darker day by day, until Cerrig could not tell the day from night; and still the fire raged on.

Finally it died. Cerrig crept out from her cave, and saw the forest ruined, twisted black and dead. The air was warm. On the shoreline of the beach, the sea crept closer. The ice-bridge had long thawed, and the other ice-islands, too, had melted into the sea.

Each day the tides grew higher, spilling into the scorched forest, flooding over the blackened stumps of trees.

That was many years ago.

Still Cerrig waits at the sea's edge, snakes her neck, breathes heat, gasping. But not fire, not again. Cerrig remembers. And waits for winter.

29

Dragoncode

Jenny Sullivan

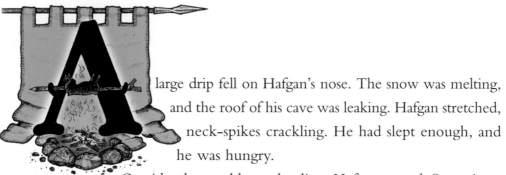

A large drip fell on Hafgan's nose. The snow was melting, and the roof of his cave was leaking. Hafgan stretched, neck-spikes crackling. He had slept enough, and he was hungry.

Outside, the world was dazzling. Hafgan roared. Sometimes his roar was fearsome, but sometimes a mighty dragonroar became more of a dragonsqueak. He kept practising. He needed to prove himself. *Especially*, he thought disgustedly, *with a name like Hafgan.* Whoever heard of a dragon called Summersong? Why couldn't he have had a name like big brothers Taran and Gwalchgwyn had? Thunder and Whitehawk. But when Hafgan had hatched, his mother had taken one look at him and, 'Aaah!' she'd said, 'isn't he *sweet!*'

At least, Hafgan consoled himself, *she's stopped calling me Dumblybumps.* When he was old enough, he had left his family and found his own cave. It was lonely sometimes, but he usually found enough to eat. Which reminded him: food.

The sea shone blue, and Hafgan plummeted into the water, surfacing seconds later with a fish clasped in his talons. It was wriggly and good, but he was still hungry. He flew inland, and his eye spotted something dark in the whiteness.

Emerging from the snow amid the rocks of the shore was a round metal object. Hafgan perched close by to observe it. It was a helmet, and as Hafgan patiently watched, a clump of snow fell, revealing an outstretched, gauntleted hand resting on the hilt of a sword.

There'll be a human inside that, Hafgan thought. Humans tasted good. But this human was probably dead, which meant that the meat would have spoiled,

30

unless the cold had kept it fresh. The biggest problem was the armour. Food was never worth it when it came in armour: it was too much trouble unwrapping it. Talons are too clumsy to undo buckles and straps, and if he munched the humans, shell and all, bits stuck between his teeth.

It probably wasn't worth the effort of lugging this human back to the cave. Hafgan spread his wings. And then the human groaned...

The hand resting on top of the sword hilt twitched. It was alive! Fresh meat! Yum!

'Help meeeee!' a creaking voice said. 'I am s-s-so cold...'

I shall soon warm you up, Hafgan thought, *and then you'll be ready to eat, all hot and crispy!*

'Pleassssse,' the voice said again, 'I imp-p-plore you in the name of all you h-h-hold dearest.'

Oh, that was so unfair! Using the Dragoncode! He had to help him now. It was his dragon duty. Hafgan opened his jaw and fastened them around the metal helmet. *One little crunch,* he thought, *and...* But he was an honourable dragon, even if he had a stupid name, and so he clasped the head gently and pulled. Not too hard. Sometimes heads came off. When the man finally creaked free, he was frozen sitting down, which made it awkward for Hafgan to fly. But he was strong for his size, and he only dropped the man once.

When he got back to his cave, Hagfan made a fire. He could have just breathed on the man in the armour, but Hafgan hadn't learned temperature control yet, and he didn't want to frizzle him after he'd saved him. Carefully, he sat the man beside the blaze, and watched him melt. Eventually, the suit sprawled sideways, and a groan came from inside the visor.

Hafgan put one golden eye close and peered in. 'Are you feeling better?' he asked.

'Oh, Gwenhwyfar's garters,' the man said, his voice echoing, 'it's a dragon. Well, that's me done for. Go on, you great, ugly brute. Crunch me up.'

'Great, ugly brute?' Hafgan repeated, furiously. 'After all I've done to rescue you, you call me names?'

'Rescue me? Is that what you call it? Picking me up by the head and dropping me, and me with the rheumatics already! Go on, finish me off.

Chew me up. All these years, and I end up a dragon's dinner,' the man said crossly, struggling into a sitting position and shoving his visor up, revealing a red face and a bristly moustache.

Ugh! A hairy face! Hafgan thought. *Disgusting.* 'But I can't eat you. You invoked the Dragoncode!' he said.

'I did what?' the man asked, unbuckling his helmet with stiff fingers.

Patiently, Hafgan reminded him, 'You said, 'I implore you in the name of all you hold dearest.' There isn't a dragon alive who could eat you after that. Just not done, eating a person who's invoked the Dragoncode. Invoking the Dragoncode means I have to take care of you forever.'

'Is that so?' The human narrowed his eyes thoughtfully. 'Is that so now? You could say I landed on my feet, couldn't you?' The man unbuckled his chest-plate and lifted it over his head. 'Phew. That's better.'

Hafgan's eyes watered. The man smelled. 'Pooh!' he said, clapping his claws across his nose. 'You're smelly!'

'What do you expect? I've been wearing this armour for months, and no chance for a bath, even if I wanted one. Don't hold with too much bathing, mind. Once a year is plenty.'

'I can tell,' Hafgan muttered. Dragons bathed at least twice a day, and sometimes took showers too when it was raining hard enough. 'Look,' he suggested, 'if I get some water, will you wash? I don't think you can stay in my cave smelling like that.'

'Is that so? Picky, picky. Well, don't think I'm washing in cold water. Hot or nothing.'

So Hafgan went and got a pot full of snow, heated it with his breath and watched as the human tested the water with his elbow.

When it was hot enough, Hafgan looked away while the human took off his stinking undergarments and washed. He was a very skinny man: Hafgan could count every one of his ribs through the pale skin. *Gracious,* he thought, *humans are ugly creatures.*

'I expect you are hungry.' said Hafgan tactfully.

'You'd be hungry, too, if you'd been stuck in ice for weeks on end,' the man grumbled.

33

Hafgan popped out to kill a small deer, and brought it back to the cave. Dragon and man sat beside the fire and roasted the meat, watching the fat drip and sizzle over the flames. Hafgan singed his a little more with his breath. He liked it overdone.

When he had finished, the man burped very loudly, rubbed his stomach, which was now rather fat, and fell over sideways.

How very rude! Hafgan thought. *Falling asleep without a story!* After supper there was always a story when there was company. And sometimes when there wasn't, because dragons carry their history in their heads, and a dragon enjoys a story told to himself just as much as one told by someone else, as it happens.

Hafgan told himself the tale of Ysbracwel, the First Dragon in the World, and when he had finished, he wrapped his tail about his head, and went to sleep.

Or tried to, because the human snored so loudly that bits of stone trickled from the cave walls, and then even louder, so that the floor trembled as if an earthquake was happening. And then to the snore was added a whistle, like steam escaping from a covered pot. And to the snore and the whistle was added a grunt and a huff. Hafgan wrapped his wings around his ears, but still the sound was unbearable.

In the morning Hafgan was so tired that he could hardly open his eyes.

The man stretched and yawned. 'I hardly slept at all!' he complained. 'I'm not a dragon, I can't sleep on a bare floor.'

Hafgan opened his mouth to frizzle the human, but shut it again. He'd promised. Frizzling wasn't allowed.

Hafgan hoped that the man would soon put on his armour and go. But he stayed and stayed, and the Dragoncode said that Hafgan had to look after him. He ate food that Hafgan caught and cooked, kept him awake all night snoring, didn't wash unless the dragon insisted, and made such a mess of Hafgan's nice, tidy cave that it almost made him want to go home to his Mam

34

and give up being grown up. The human's manners were dreadful, and his personal habits... well, they put Hafgan right off his food.

Summer came, and the man got smellier still. Hafgan suggested a swim, since the weather was warm, but the man refused. 'What are you trying to do to me?' he asked. 'Ruins your skin, getting wet! Makes it shrink!'

'But—' Hafgan began, then gave up. The man was not to be persuaded. Poor Hafgan wished he'd never set eyes on him. His life was utterly miserable.

One hot summer's day, the smell was so bad that Hafgan was driven to desperation. He picked up the smelly, sweaty, hairy – and by now much fatter – human by the scruff of his neck and dangled him out in the fresh air for five minutes.

'Oy! Put me down!' the human shouted. 'I invoked the Dragoncode! You've got to do what I say!'

Hafgan ignored him. Fresh air was not enough. He carried him down to the river, and dropped him in. The man floundered and spat, and the water all around him turned a curious muddy colour. He said some very rude words and accused Hafgan of breaking his oath. But at least he would be clean for a while, Hafgan thought.

The man scrambled to the bank. 'You'll pay for this, dragon!' he screamed. 'You'll feed me well for this, you will. I invoked the Dragoncode, I did. You have to look after me for ev–'

Something very large swooped down and scooped the human up from the riverbank. A swirl of crimson wings, snap, crunch, munch and gollop and the dreadful, smelly, noisy human had gone forever.

'Ha, little brother!' Hafgan's big brother Taran roared. 'Keeping a delicious tastybit all to yourself? Greedy boy! Serves you right! Now I've eaten it! That'll teach you to hoard food! Ha!'

'But –!' Hafgan began, meaning to tell his brother that the human had invoked the Dragoncode and that Taran had committed a terrible Dragonsin. Then he stopped. And smiled to himself. What did their grand-dragon used to say when she wanted a bit of peace? Least said, soonest mended.

'You rotter!' he roared back. 'I'm telling Mam on you! You pinched my lunch, you did!'

35

Elgar and the Dragons

Christine Evans

In the far north-west of Wales, at the end of a long arm of green land, there is an island. It rises like a sleeping whale, turning its back to the mainland, making it a mysterious, beckoning place. Small enough to walk round in half a day, big enough to hide away for a whole afternoon, the island is a small, secret world where, even today, there are caves that only the birds and the grey seals know. For thousands of years, it was one of the places where the Dragon-kind, who live most of their lives in air or water and rarely put their trust in earth, came to nest in the big gorse bushes ablaze with golden blossom. There they would raise their young until they were old enough to fly. Some returned here to die, their bones not surviving as skeletons but dissolving back into dust in a single, searing instant.

When the human beings came, it took a long time for them to learn how to see dragons – for though they are made out of the same stuff as we are, in them the atoms dance to a different pattern, so to our eyes they look like shimmery air. It is like staring through the flame of a very hot bonfire, or into a thin ripple of rainbow colours, swirling as oil-spills do in a puddle. These creatures are as real and almost as invisible as breeze quivering the leaves. But once people learned to look sideways out of the corners of their eyes and glimpsed tails and horns and spiky heads that sometimes breathed flame, they panicked and called them 'devils'. Fear spreads faster than a forest fire, and so the dragons were driven out, further and further west.

36

To our island came two adults, travelling on passage with their hatchling, sailing the wind with wings widespread ahead of a gathering storm. This clench of rock and fertile soil was named in their legends as the Rock of the Morloi – 'the calves of the sea', as they called the seals. It was known in past times as a stopover on the long flight to the big Island of the Lakes whose far blue mountains can still be glimpsed across the ocean as the sun goes down. Cliffs white with crowding birds showed them that there would be rich fishing-grounds nearby, and so they decided to sit out the storm in a huge cave. First Daedal and then Aurea folded their huge wings and crept under the overhanging rock, followed by their son (not yet named by a Gathering, although he had seen his tenth winter).

There was a chorus of snorts and splashes as the full-fed seals lounging on the shelves of red rock lurched and slid noisily into the water. Only when they felt safe outside the cave did they dare turn to look at what had woken them. To them, the Dragon-kind were monsters, sharks of the air, but in his long life, Daedal had met *morloi* before and knew that, though they could not understand his words, his voice would soothe and colour their thoughts. He would show them that he and his family meant them no harm. So, in former times, were all earth's creatures linked.

Next day, the storm past, the three flew together over the island, diving for fish and grazing on the dark red seaweed. The hatchling was entranced by the brightness of the sea-pinks, and tried to eat gorse flowers because he thought they looked like yellow sparks. They saw a white-haired two-legs far below, but one alone was no threat to them, and anyway, they were sure he would not be able to see them clearly.

People had lived on the island since before the sea rose and cut it off from the mainland, but at the time of this story many hundreds of years ago, there was only Elgar, the last of many holy men who had chosen the island as a place to pray and feel close to God. He was old now, and his life had been hard and adventurous: kidnapped by pirates as a boy, he had been a slave for years until he escaped on a ship that sank near the island. The brother monks saved him from the waves. It was five years since he had blessed the last of his companions and buried him in the little green plot next to the church.

38

Five years of no other voice except the bird calls and the long wailing of the seals from the rocks. And five years of living on what few vegetables he could grow in the salty wind, what he could find or catch on the shore – in winter, only handfuls of winkles, small grey lumps of gristle.

He began, that spring, to feel he was no longer on his own, that someone else was nearby, just out of sight on the path as he paced back to his hut high on the hill. Stepping outside to say his morning prayers he felt a disturbance in the air, like a tremble of wings vast as clouds, and sometimes at night, vague luminous shapes moved across the stars. At once he thought of angel messengers, but he also knew that he was so hungry, perhaps his eyes were playing tricks on him. So, taking his stoutest hazel stick, he went out into in the cold, bright wind of early March to see if the gulls had come back to their nest-sites high above the sea and could spare an egg or two. He was clambering stiffly along the ledge when suddenly the ground gave way and he was tumbling through earth and tangled roots and jumbled red stone into a sea cave vaulted like a cathedral, with one light-filled opening to the waves.

Pain lanced his crumpled leg, and colours danced all about him, strange sounds like flutes and cymbals hissing in his ears before his world went dark.

He woke to grey light in the damp, cold cave and vast shadows twisting round him, their deep calls weaving into a ringing tune. When he tried to sit up, his leg felt numb and heavy. Then he felt his arms gripped, as if by steel claws, and he was lifted and swung out low over the open sea (and here he squeezed his eyes shut against the memory of shipwreck and the terror of near-drowning). He was swooshed through the air and bumped down in soft grass. Cautiously, he opened his eyes.

He was lying outside his own hut high on the hill, among the warm, scented gorse, and three tall shapes flickering like flames were lifting off into a calm blue sky.

He lay where they had left him, gazing up as their rich colours faded. He sipped from the bowl of fresh water left within reach and then drowsed gently with the sun on his face. He dreamed he was back in his mother's kitchen on baking day. And woke to find his nostrils full of the fragrance of warm bread – a loaf, fresh from the oven, crisp-crusted, sat on a rock beside him. It was one of three left on a windowsill to cool that the young dragon had seen and, in a daring swoop, snatched and carried high across the white-capped waves. To Elgar it was miraculous: water sprang into his mouth so he could hardly murmur a quick grace. As he chewed, he felt his strength returning.

Next day, a long silver fish lay on the rock with three turnips, and a bundle of dry sticks for his fire. Then there were duck eggs, an end of hard cheese and once, part of a deer's leg, left after a rich man's hunting. The dragons could fly high and far; they brought him what they could, and slowly, his leg healed. One afternoon as he sat bathing it in cold water beside the well he heard a strange bleating call, and there was a brown-and-white goat, a nanny with an udder full of milk. Elgar was delighted, but puzzled by the goat's sudden appearance. He could not know that she had strayed from the flock searching for the sweetest grass, had jumped right down to the rocks as goats will, and got herself trapped just above the sea. She would surely have drowned when the tide rose if the hatchling had not seen her, and fetched his father to carry her across to the island.

Now Elgar was content. Every day brought him a new wonder. Often the young dragon would stay beside him for a while and he heard the ringing tune that he knew to be a sort of talk. If you have ever heard whales singing, or the stretched-out humming of an old bronze bowl, struck lightly, or rain driven against a huge church bell until the clapper trembles – that is how the dragon-language sounded in Elgar's grateful ears. And gradually, he began to understand a little. Not in words, but through the colour of his thoughts he recognised a fellow living creature, innocent and brave, who had a care for him but would soon have to leave.

'Our long lives are spent
sailing the wind, piercing the deep, green depths;
only rarely resting upon earth.

So many two-legs now, too many of their roads,
their fighting;
they have felled the forests, spread their towns
across the hills which hid us once.

Even the seas are busy with their boats.
Soon, not even the depths
will be safe for us, our kind.
We must keep moving, westward, further out
to other islands, green places
where there will be lakes and hills,
caves for all of us and sanctuary, perhaps.
We only stayed to see you safe.'

All Elgar could see was a moving moony sheen, a tall shape shot through with shimmering turquoise, navy and magenta. The legend says he put out a hand towards it, and touched the neck of the boy-dragon: scales, cool as silver, made a smoothly interlocking mesh, gently rippling.

He said a simple blessing and stood back, leaning on his stick. He was smiling but tears stood in his eyes as he felt the beat of giant wings and one last flute-note of farewell. In his hand was a clutch of tiny bright discs, purple as the petals of a foxglove, shiny as a prince's armour.

For seven more years he lived alone, as a hermit, even though he was visited by other men of the church who begged him to leave. His story of the angel-visions and their heavenly voices became famous and has kept his name alive for ten centuries. He had a simple life with few comforts, but at least he had enough to eat: the birds gathered and brought him seeds and berries, and sometimes apples from mainland orchards; each high tide the seals would leave a fresh-caught fish; and the nanny goat and the mischievous kid she produced were company, even when the milk supply dried up.

What became of the dragons? Well, that is a different story.

There is another legend of the island: that where dragondust lies thickest above the jasper cave, the sea-pinks grow brighter, and at night, they shimmer like a drift of stars.

41

Gorse Gold and Shell Blue

Gaye Hicyilmaz

My elder brother, Owen, cleared our lower field all by himself. He worked on it day after day and week after week, tearing off the golden gorse. The land was too rough for the sort of plough you'd hitch behind a horse. He'd used a breast plough which he'd strapped against his chest. Then, hour after hour he'd driven that plough up the slope. He'd forced the iron blade against the rocks and he'd torn his way through the roots. I'd followed, raking up what was left and trying to clear the stones. I'd longed to be strong enough and tall enough to do his work, but I wasn't, then, so I'd watched. Sometimes, I'd had to lean on the rake to catch my breath and when I couldn't bear to watch his struggle any longer, I'd looked out over the endless brightness of the sea instead. Behind me, he'd carried on, forcing his way through the silent, close-packed earth. In the evening, when he'd washed, I'd seen the mark the plough had made on his chest.

Neighbours had also watched but they hadn't ever helped. They'd said that the task was impossible and that he was an ignorant youth. When he succeeded, they laughed. That land was too near the sea, they said. The sea and the salt spray would ruin any crops. But they didn't. We put seaweed on the land and it grew the best field of oats that anyone round here has ever

42

had. In the autumn I'd helped Mam tread the oatmeal down into our chest and that year, for the first time ever, we'd filled it up to the brim. At the end of that winter, we'd given bowlfuls away to neighbours who hadn't enough.

In the spring the landlord's agent rode by to collect in the rents. He'd asked for my brother and I'd pointed to the beach where Owen was gathering seaweed to put on the new land. The agent frowned. Could he get there on horseback, he asked. I laughed at him then. Didn't he even know about the cliffs? Didn't he realise that when Owen and I collected seaweed, we clambered on all fours, with the baskets tied on our backs?

The agent had scowled at my bare feet and shrugged.

'How old are you?' he'd asked.

I'd scowled at his polished boots and this time I'd shrugged back.

'Well,' he'd said, 'when you're taller and needing work, tell your mother to bring you up to the big house. If they need a girl in the kitchens, and if you're a good worker, they might offer you a job.'

Owen had patted my hand when I'd told him.

'My little sister? Their servant?' He'd said and he'd laughed.

A week later a boy came from the big house, carrying a note. On account of the improvements we'd made to the farm, the landlord was putting up our rent. Mam wept. Owen's face changed so much that I thought he'd seen a ghost. Then, while I was collecting seaweed on the beach, Owen suddenly left. Mam said that he was going to the valleys. He'd join the miners digging out the coal. He'd save the rent money from his wages and send it with someone who was travelling our way. In the meantime Mam and I should carry on as best we could.

That day I carried up six loads. The next day I was so exhausted I couldn't manage one. I had to tip half out before I could climb on. Each dawn we watched for someone passing through and each dusk marked the end of another hopeless day when neither news nor money came to help us out.

In the autumn the agent returned for the rent. When Mam told him that she couldn't pay, he'd looked me up and down, but taken chickens against the debt. That winter Mam got her cough. When spring came, and she was a little better, she made me wash my dress. Then we followed the long road

43

up to the landlord's house. The housekeeper inspected my mouth and hair and said I smelt of fish. I corrected her. It wasn't fish. Without Owen, Mam and me weren't strong enough to launch the boat. Nowadays our only catch was the crabs I found amongst the weed and rocks. Mam silenced me with a look. Then she apologised for the fishy smell and agreed that the landlord needn't pay me for my work. Whatever I earned must be set against the debt. But, on the first Sunday of each month, I can go home to the farm, so long as I'm back in the landlord's house before dark.

And that's all I think about when I'm carrying their jugs of hot water up to their rooms, or scrubbing their blackened pans with the ash from their grates. Sometimes, if it's wet on Sundays, they won't let me leave.

'It's for your own good,' they say. 'A soaking will only leave you chilled and weak.'

Then, I watch the rain soaking in to their smooth, green lawns, and wait for another month to pass.

Today, however, is a fine Sunday. It's hot and still and bright. I should think I've been walking for an hour at least. My body is wet under their scratchy dress and their cast-off boots would have rubbed my feet raw if I hadn't taken them off and hung them round my neck.

But I'm here: another six steps and I'm home. There's the field that Owen cleared. The gorse and the brambles are growing back. There's the breast plough, where he flung it, on that pile of stones. There's our cottage, with the door still shut. I drop their boots onto our step. Through the window I can see Mam on the bed. It must be past midday but I think I'll let her rest. I unbutton their dress and stand there in my shift. I've never known it to be so hot. Carefully, I lift the seaweed basket from its peg under the eaves and I fasten its rope round my waist.

Now I'm scrambling down the cliff. This is our old path to the beach. When I look back at the cottage a raven is floating in the hot air, watching me from above.

The tide is so far out. The rocks are uncovered as far as I can see. The banks of mussels are like the black buds of sky-blue flowers that will only bloom beneath the waves. The seaweed glistens and slips. It's as smooth as their

44

carpets and it's gentle and cool under my burning feet. Now, I untie the rope. I don't know why I brought the basket, except that it's what we always did. I stretch up into the still air and I feel the sun touching my skin underneath.

I'm making my way over the rocks to a place where the sea is dark and cold and deep. I think of Owen in the mine. I can see him crouching there, covered in dust, driving in his pick. I close my eyes, but the sun is so strong that it burns right through my lids. Up in the cottage Mam will have woken, won't she? She'll be feeling better and getting up.

A shadow wings across my face. I listen for the raven's croak and when I don't hear it, I look up.

And see what can't be there. I duck. It's a winged and tailed thing that's swooping and leaping and floating and gliding in the brilliant summer air. It's flying in from the sea. It's as gold as the flowers on the gorse and as blue as the mussel shells. Its eyes are steady and cool but I think there's fire in its mouth. As it flaps its butterfly-patterned wings I can feel the breeze on my face. It's beautiful to watch. I shield my eyes. It's the blue of bluebells and the yellow of dandelions in the grass and it's more beautiful than anything I've ever seen. I blink. And when I look again I see more and more of them, swooping and diving and rushing past, where I've never seen them before. My cold heart lifts. Behind me, the raven croaks, but my creatures are swift and silent as my thoughts.

The tide has turned. I climb back up the cliff. Now that I know these creatures are near me, I don't turn round to look. I pass the still closed door. The breast plough is there on the pile of stones. I heave it into the basket so that it will not scar my back. I leave their dress and their boots on the ground. I'll only wear my shift.

As I press on towards the landlord's house, the clouds are piling up. By the time I've reached their wall, I've felt the first fat drops. Now the rain is falling like waves. I'm crouching on the edge of their wood. Their stream has overflowed and is running over my feet. I'm alone, but I'm not afraid. I understand that creatures like that must return to their homes on the shore. Up here they could not have flown freely. Their butterfly wings would have been trapped and torn amongst these great, green trees.

Now, I'm happy to wait. And when the night is dark and black and thick, I take the breast plough from the basket and I walk across their lawn. I hold my breath and lean into the metal. The blade sinks in and tears up their softened grass. I work all night. And as I'm leaving in the morning I hear them crying in terror, that a dragon's been across.

47

The Cathedral Dragon

Nona Rees

There is a little room, high up in the tower of St Davids Cathedral. It is perfectly round. Today, nobody knows where it is. A dim light filters in from a tiny arched window, high up in the wall. The room is empty except for a pinkish-grey stone with a funny bumpy surface, but it's not a stone, it's a dragon, and dust has settled on his bright red scales.

When he is not busy, the cathedral dragon sleeps. He dreams of the great lord Merlin who came to see him when he had just hatched from his egg. Dragon and wizard looked at each other and in a voice of whispering leaves, Merlin spoke.

'Aha! A pedigree red long-neck. I don't see many of these nowadays. I name you Dafydd. You will have a really important task. A very special baby has been born, in the Land of the Setting Sun. You will forever guard this boy child and his chosen place.'

So when Dafydd the Dragon grew up and learned to breathe fire, which took about a week (they grow very fast), he set out for the Land where the Sun falls off the rim of the world into the sea and he watched over David, the great Saint of Wales. Long ago, there were many dragons around and most were friendly. The people of St Davids would leave dragon cakes out, made with a special recipe of fish, snails, special herbs and crushed crab shells, fried in butter, which Dafydd really loved.

Dafydd kept watch over St David for the whole of his long life on earth. And after the saint died, Dafydd had to look after the great cathedral that stood in Glyn Rhosyn, St David's chosen place. For some centuries, all was quiet. But everything was about to change.

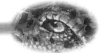

'C'mon. Wake up, lazy! It's half-past-six, you should have been up half an hour ago.'

'Mmmm. Oh, stop it! Leave me alone.'

It was the usual morning scene in the Prothero household. Padrig was up with the lark and Ffion was a small, determined lump under the blankets and eiderdown. Mr and Mrs Prothero farmed Pen Clegyr on the hill above the cathedral. Before school, it was Ffion's job to feed the chickens and collect the eggs and Padrig helped with milking the cows.

But it was wartime and although life went on much the same at Pen Clegyr, enemy aeroplanes were dropping bombs on Milford Haven and Pembroke Dock.

'Mam, suppose they drop bombs on St Davids,' said Ffion.

Mam smiled. 'Now why would they want to do that, bach? We haven't got anything they'd want to bomb, like factories or big ships.'

Many aeroplanes flew over St Davids and Padrig knew all their names: Halifaxes, Liberators and Flying Fortresses. The aerodrome was near his school and when planes took off, all work had to stop. The roar was deafening and the whole building shook.

'They're part of Coastal Command,' he told a wide-eyed Ffion, 'and protect all our coastline.'

Dafydd the Dragon stirred in his sleep. Something felt very wrong. His golden eyes opened, large dragon ears pricked up. In a long, thin, magic streak, he slithered out through the little arched window and flew, silent and invisible round the cathedral and the city. At night, darkness was everywhere − not a single light showed. Dafydd was uneasy.

In the evenings, the Prothero family would gather round the radio to listen to the latest news. On this particular evening, a flat, nasal voice announced, 'Germany calling! Germany calling'. It was a man called Lord Haw Haw, who broadcast for the enemy on British radio.

'Don't you go believing everything this man says,' said John Prothero and then he stopped and held his breath.

'I have a message for you, people of St Davids,' announced Lord Haw

49

Haw. 'I have visited your peninsula and know it very well. We are going to bomb your cathedral tonight. In the morning not one wall will be left standing.'

Ffion began to cry, her mother was white as a sheet and held the little girl tightly. 'There, there cariad, don't cry. Mami and Dad will keep you safe.'

Padrig, fear prickling his scalp, looked at his father.

'We've got to do something, quick!' said John Prothero. 'I'm going to round up the men.'

'Can I come too?' cried Padrig.

'No, boy, you must stay with Mam and Ffion. You're the man of the house now.'

Disappointed, Padrig watched his father put on his heavy coat and hurry away into the night. From the doorway of Pen Clegyr Padrig could just make out the dark shape of *his* cathedral, where he sang in the choir. A lump came to his throat, but he was too angry to cry.

Unknown to the family, just outside the window, a dragon had been listening too. Dafydd knew that this might be his most difficult task. He could not let down the great Saint of Wales at this dark and dangerous time.

Suddenly, Padrig saw two golden eyes, like dim lamps glowing in the darkness. He heard a soft swish and something very like a long, scaly tail flicked around his feet. He should have been terrified, but instead, he felt rather excited. Was it the dragon his grandparents used to talk about, who was supposed to live in the cathedral?

The dragon watched the boy and then said in his softest, kindest hiss, 'Can you help me save the cathedral?'

'Oh *yes*!' whispered Padrig. 'Are you the cathedral dragon?'

'Yesss,' hissed Dafydd. 'A flying steel dragon will try and destroy the cathedral tonight, but I don't know which of these man-made dragons is an enemy.'

'Oh *I* do,' whispered Padrig. 'They're not real dragons. They are aeroplanes and I can easily tell which ones are the enemy.'

'You can come with me then,' hissed Dafydd. 'Later this night. It's quite easy. I have a little pouch under my wing. You'll be quite safe.'

Padrig nearly burst with excitement. 'Can you hover under my bedroom window when I go to bed and I'll tap when I'm ready?'

50

First, though, he had to pretend he was cross and grumpy at having to stay at home.

'Come on, Padrig, try not to worry,'said Mam. 'All the men are on watch and Dad will tell you all about it in the morning. Off to bed with you now, there's a good boy.'

Padrig stumped upstairs, put his pyjamas on over his clothes and got into bed. He waited till Mam's bedroom door clicked shut and then crept over to the window. He tapped. There, hovering, was a huge scaly back. Balancing carefully on the narrow window sill, Padrig climbed on to Dafydd's shoulder and from there slipped easily round and down into the dragon's pouch. It was surprisingly dry and warm.

'Ready to go?' hissed Dafydd.

'Oh, yes!' said Padrig.

Then began the night of his life, as he sat tucked into the warm pouch, sheltered by Dafydd's huge wing. As they flew over the silent city, Padrig peeped out. Far below, people were lugging sandbags, hoses and water pumps towards the cathedral.

'What are you going to do?' asked Padrig.

'I will breathe dragonfire and raise a mist that will come up from the river and hide the cathedral,' promised Dafydd solemnly.

Even as the dragon spoke, there came the drone of aircraft from only a short distance away. Dafydd reared up and hissed his alarm in a plume of flame.

'No! No! That's not enemy aircraft,' shouted Padrig. 'It's a Flying Fortress – I know by the sound. It's on the lookout, protecting us, like you!'

'Hold tight,' commanded Dafydd. In a tight circle, he dived gracefully, down close to the cathedral tower, and watched as the American aircraft passed overhead. On the nose of the craft, the pilots had painted a fiery beast and given her a grand name – Dragonora. It was almost as though they had always known that they would one day meet a real dragon. But dragons are cleverer than aeroplanes and there was no time to lose. Already, Padrig could make out the distant throbbing of enemy planes.

'Now, Dafydd,' urged Padrig. 'The mist! These are the bombers!'

Padrig felt the great dragon body start to shudder. It became hotter and

52

hotter. Below, the mist swirled like steam from a great boiler, covering the whole valley. Padrig hid right at the bottom of his safe pouch, too frightened to look.

Then suddenly, BROOOMMMMM. The air quivered, the earth shuddered as a bomb exploded. Throb, throb, throb, went the powerful engines, and again, BROOOMMMMM, as another bomb struck the still trembling earth.

Padrig didn't dare look out. Suppose – it was too awful – there was no cathedral. Suppose his father was dead. He hated this horrible war. His throat felt tight. Hot tears pricked his eyelids.

Dafydd felt the boy's little body tighten in his pouch. 'Don't worry, Padrig,' he hissed softly. 'All will be well – just wait and see!'

Padrig peered cautiously out of the pouch at the land below. He could see two fires raging, but they were far apart, one each side of the Valley. Slowly, the mist melted away, and there was the tower and the dear old cathedral, all unharmed. The brave people of St Davids were going home to their beds.

The bombs had fallen on two farmhouses. No one was even hurt, though Mr and Mrs Evans had their farmhouse cut in half, right through the bedroom wall. The firemen found them still in bed, too terrified to move.

And Padrig? Well, Dafydd the dragon slipped him silently back into his bedroom before he vanished back into his tower. Padrig snuggled down under the bedclothes, and was asleep in seconds.

When he woke up in the morning, he rubbed his eyes extra hard. Dragonora. The mist. The bombing. Had he just been dreaming?

Downstairs, Mam and Dad were both excited.

'Well, Padrig, what a night!' said his father.

'Go on,' urged Mam, 'Tell him what happened!'

But Padrig realised that he already knew everything his father knew – and more. So it couldn't have been a dream, could it?

53

The Fire Offering

Peter Oram

Gareth banged the door, hard. He hoped his parents would hear it slam and tell him to come back and get on with his homework. But they were too busy arguing. They were always arguing these days. And what had Dad just said? Something about leaving for good? Gareth wasn't sure. He'd tried to block his ears, and when that didn't help he knew he had to get out.

He walked down the hill to the bridge, where a large seagull on a post greeted him with squawking laughter.

'Get lost!' he yelled at it as he passed, and it rose into the air on heavy wings and slid away. Gareth climbed the hill on the other side and reached the High Street. The shops were already closing. The last few people were drifting off home, the last cars humming by and turning out of sight. A cold wind began to blow towards him. He passed the chippie on the corner. Its windows were dark and lifeless. Only the sour smell of vinegar still clung to the air. Glancing down the street to the left he saw, hanging low in the slate-grey sky, the sun, smouldering with a dull red glow, the embers of a forgotten fire. He shivered. Everything around him seemed to be darkening, fading, dying. He felt cold and empty. He would have cried, but he didn't

54

have any tears left. He wanted to go home.

He turned and began to walk back down the High Street, but stopped half-way along it. Home? The place that had once been home didn't seem to want him now. He turned off to the left down Priory Street. Not a soul in sight, and no one saw him as he reached the darkened doorway to a shop and slipped into the safety of its shadows.

He sat for a long time without moving on the cold stone. Only once did he crane his neck to look out and up along the street. On the gabled wall of the Guildhall tower he could just make out the flag, fluttering nervously in the dim light of the street lamp. For some reason it seemed to comfort him a little.

There must have been hundreds of them, for they covered almost completely the steep green slopes. Here they were safe and unseen. The valley was closed in on three sides; a part of the wild, bare hills had been gouged out to form a giant cauldron, broken open on the fourth side where the moors stretched away into the distance. A chaotic tumble of rocks and boulders straddled the great curve of its rim, forming a natural barrier between the valley and the world outside. Any passing wanderer attempting to climb over to see what lay beyond would soon give up and walk on, never suspecting the secret meeting-place within. As for the open side, no one ever ventured onto the moors anyway, for the bogs were many and treacherous.

For a long time all were silent. They'd come from far and wide, and were anxious to learn why they'd been called so urgently. But they were travel-weary too, and content to rest a little first.

He sat amongst them, wondering how he'd got there. And wondering what had happened to his hands. They were his, yet they were different in some way. unfamiliar. Was it the coarse, red skin? The long nails, curved and horny? He couldn't work it out. He gave up, and raised his eyes to look out across the valley.

Opposite him, high on a rock, sat Yzmer, oldest and wisest of all, casting his sad eyes over the crowd, counting. They were all here. Yzmer raised himself up to his full height and spoke.

'Few of you will know why I have summoned you, though some may

55

have guessed...' He paused and sighed, and flame shot out from his jaws, '...but every one of you – even little Yzmettiz over there...'

Yzmettiz? Was his name Yzmettiz? Of course it was!... but wasn't it also something else, something quite different? But what? Though he searched deep in his memory, he found nothing. Had he dreamt something?

'...even little Yzmettiz knows who first gave us, when we were new and young in the world, the things we prize most – our fire, our strength, our wisdom...'

A soft and reverent murmur went through the crowd –

'The sun! … it was the sun.'

'Yes, yes! The sun! But now...' and a still more mournful look entered Yzmer's eye, 'the time has come to repay that debt, for...' He paused again, for so long that little Yzmettiz (who had just remembered his dream and what his name had been in it) began to giggle. But Yzmer, hearing him even from the far slope, silenced him with a brief, piercing glance, and then came to the point:

'...for the sun,' he said, 'is dying.'

A cry of disbelief and dismay arose from the crowd. Even Yznwl, the Sleepy One, was wide awake. He flailed his wings angrily, almost knocking over those on either side of him:

'Dying? *Dying?* Who dared let this happen? Who caused this calamity? I say we seek out these traitors! Destroy them!'

'Silence, Yznwl. Calm yourself. This isn't the time for lost tempers and hasty deeds. There's no single culprit. For hundreds of years all the good things that men and women do on the earth – helping one another, creating beautiful things, building friendships between countries and peoples – have been the fuel that the sun needs to burn. In return, the sun has given its great light and warmth. But in later years people have changed. They fight amongst themselves, become selfish, greedy, and whole countries have made war with one another, causing great suffering...'

'Yznwl was right!' cried Yzbellik the fearless. 'We must find the rogues and kill them!'

'Impossible,' said Yzmer, 'It's not one person, but thousands, hundreds

of thousands, millions even.' He sighed out another long flame. 'The trouble is, the cycle has been broken: since there's now so little good to fuel the sun, it has ever less power to send light and warmth to the earth, and hearts turn cold as darkness enters. We must act, now, to restore the balance.'

Twin forks of flame shot out of Yzbellik's nostrils, blackening the grass before him.

'To battle!' he roared. 'We'll stop this rot at its source!' With three powerful wingbeats he rose into the air, spinning around with a dramatic flourish before returning to his perch.

'To battle! To battle!' echoed the crowd.

But Yzmer said quietly:, 'No.'

The crowd fell silent.

'... no, that would only add more violence, more evil. We must think of something else.'

They thought long and hard, murmuring amongst themselves all the while. At last little Yzmettit said in a soft, shy voice:

'*We* all have fire, every one of us. If we were to put all our fire together and give it to the sun, then perhaps...'

That was all Yzmer heard, since the rest of the crowd, quick to forget the seriousness of it all, were already hooting with laughter. But he'd heard enough, and he cried out in such a loud voice that they all shut up immediately:

'The youngster's right. This plan I, too, had in mind, but hoped one of you would voice it. For it may mean the end of us, and I didn't want to carry the responsibility for that on my own. But this young member of our clan has come up with it all by himself, putting the rest of us to shame. And since none of you has anything better to offer, I suggest we do as he says.'

'But how?' protested several of them at once.

'It will be dangerous. Many of us will not return. Maybe none. For a great sacrifice will be required of us. To give our fire to the sun we must race with it a whole day on its journey to the west. Even though it is dying, its heat will be too great during the day for us to get close enough. But we can do so in the evening, as it sets. Then, when I give the sign, we shall all blow into it, emptying our lungs of flame. The sun will burst into life again,

and people on earth will return to peaceful and harmonious ways...' He paused and then, in a voice that was suddenly very quiet, he added, 'but we, in the enormous flames that spring out to us from the new-born sun – we... will burn immediately to ashes. There will be no more dragons in Wales. Unless any of you lack the courage to follow me...'

For a long time no one spoke a word. At last Yzlind the Fair, who had been sitting all the while just behind little Yzmettit, said:

'I do not lack the courage, Yzmer, nor, I am sure, does little Yzmettit here. But he surely lacks the strength for such a journey.'

'Well said, dear Yzlind. Yzmettit shall remain here. Perhaps he will find tasks of similar importance during the three thousand or so years of his life that lie ahead.' He rattled his wings and slapped his huge, barbed tail on the rock behind him like a whip, and concluded: 'Very well. It is agreed. We leave tomorrow at dawn.'

Before sunrise the whole flock was in the air, circling far above the valley on whirring wings. But still higher up, much higher, little Yzmettit drifted back and forth, his eyes filled with tears. He would have gladly made the sacrifice too, he wasn't afraid of dying in spite of his few years, but they were right – he wouldn't have been able to fly so far and fast. Yzmer had agreed that little Yzmettit should accompany them as far as the coast, and he had flown high above them to get the best view of his flockmates for the last time. How beautiful they looked now as the rim of the sun lit up like a diamond on the eastern horizon. Hundreds moving as one, they turned themselves away from it and, in perfectly spaced formation, set off on their journey to meet it that evening when it would

lower its red-glowing ball into the cool blue skies of the west. How graceful they looked to little Yzmettit, looking down on them as they gathered speed, the red of their scaly bodies bright against the lush green fields of West Wales far below.

By the time they reached the rugged coast he was already too tired to keep up. He hovered a while, watching them sadly as they sped off into the distance. Slowly, he made his way back to the valley, crawled under a rock and closed his eyes, and tried to imagine the glorious sunrise that was to come. As he recalled the great courage of his vanished flock he was filled with pride, and comforted by this, he fell asleep.

Gareth was woken by the rattle of bottles on a passing milk van. He was freezing cold and stiff all over. He must have been dreaming. For a few moments he couldn't even remember his own name, let alone where he was.

He peered out of the doorway and looked up the empty street. The Guildhall clock said a quarter to six. He shifted his gaze to the flag. At that very moment the whole street was suddenly transformed, filled with an incredible, brilliant light. At first Gareth couldn't understand it, and in any case it was so bright that he couldn't open his eyes. But at last he did so: the morning sun had just risen, sending its broad, brilliant beam up along the full length of the street. The flag on the Guildhall danced and fluttered in the new light, and the red dragon on it seemed to be alive, and dancing too.

Gareth stood up, stretched, and began to walk home. His sadness and loneliness were gone. He somehow knew that things would be all right from now on. His parents would stop squabbling, his dad would take time off work and stop 'overdoing it' as his mum always said he did, and in the summer they would all go on holiday together. Yes, it was going to be all right.

By the time he reached the street where he lived, he was running.

The
Village that
Lost its Dragon

Phil Carradice

Boy lived in a village right on the sea's edge in Pembrokeshire. Boy had a name, of course, a real name, but nobody used it. Everybody called him Boy because when he was born he was the only male child in the village. There were other children, but they were all girls and called by their proper names. Boy was just Boy – and always would be.

The village was ordinary enough; a few houses around the harbour, a beach where fishing boats were painted – and, of course, the dragon.

Boy was five when he saw the dragon for the first time. He and his father were walking to school when a sudden movement on the cliff above the harbour caught his eye.

'Look!' Boy called. 'What's that?'

'Only Cyfarthfa,' said his father.

There was a roar as something huge swept out from the cliff towards them. Boy heard its wings creaking like a swan's as the creature passed overhead and he watched in amazement.

'Cyfarthfa's a dragon,' smiled his father. 'He lives here; has done for a thousand years.'

The dragon's scales were blue and white and his huge opal eyes, round as marbles, stared at them for a moment before he swept on over the sea.

61

As Boy grew older he became used to seeing Cyfarthfa. Sometimes he would catch a glimpse of the dragon on the cliff path; other times he would see him sweeping like a giant bat out of the sunset. At night Boy would gaze up at the stars and see the shape of Cyfarthfa, silent and magical as a dream, against the darkened sky. He never spoke to the dragon, never quite summoned up the courage, but he was proud that Cyfarthfa lived in his village.

Unfortunately, not everyone felt the same.

'He's a menace!'

Boy was dawdling at the harbour, watching the brightly-coloured boats while Dai Jones, the fisherman, talked to his father and the other men.

'He's always stealing our fish,' Dai growled, 'before we even get them out of the nets. If you ask me it's time he moved on. The day of the dragon is over.'

Boy's father shook his head.

'Come on, Dai, a few fish never hurt anyone. Live and let live. That dragon's been part of this village for years.'

'Really?' Dai Jones sneered, his mouth cruel and dark, like a wound across his face.

'Then it's about time he went elsewhere. And if he won't go willingly perhaps we should make him.'

Boy and his father walked home. Neither of them spoke until they reached their cottage.

'Why does Dai hate Cyfarthfa, Dad?' Boy asked.

His father shrugged. 'Some people are like that. They hate what they don't understand, hate anything that's different. Dai Jones? He's just frightened. The fishing's been pretty bad lately.'

One winter afternoon Boy was walking beside the bay when the swish of Cyfarthfa's wings made him glance up in alarm. The dragon was heading towards a small fishing boat at the mouth of the harbour. With a sinking feeling Boy realised that the boat was Dai Jones's *Pelican*. Boy could see fish splashing and leaping around the hull – Dai had found a good catch at last.

'No, Cyfarthfa!' Boy called but his words were lost in the wind.

He watched as the dragon dipped his wings and dived towards the shoal

of fish. Or did he? Suddenly Boy realised that Cyfarthfa wasn't after the fish at all – he was after the net. Dai Jones was so busy pulling in his catch, gloating over his good luck, that he hadn't seen his danger. *Pelican* was being dragged steadily towards the rocks at the harbour mouth. Another minute and she would be ashore.

'Fly, Cyfarthfa!' yelled Boy. 'Fly!'

The dragon dropped like a stone. With his giant talons he seized the net. There was a loud ripping sound, like fabric tearing, and the net suddenly appeared on the surface of the water. Then it was in the air, a rope bridge between the dragon and the boat. Boy heard Dai Jones cry out as his boat was lifted ten feet into the air. Fish poured out of the net, falling in a silver cascade into the sea.

'Help!' cried the frightened fisherman.

Cyfarthfa swung around and with a huge splash the boat was back in the water. With a few strong, steady wing-beats, Cyfarthfa towed *Pelican* safely into harbour, then with a shake of his talons, he dropped the net. He was free now to soar back into the sky, where he circled once and then glided away to his cave in the cliff. Boy shook his head in wonderment at the creature's feat.

At the harbour wall, a crowd had gathered to help Dai out of his battered boat.

'Did you see?' he demanded. 'The dragon tried to kill me. It's the final straw – he's got to go.'

Several villagers nodded and Boy knew he should speak out and tell them what really happened. But before he could open his mouth, Dai was dragged away towards the village pub and Boy was left alone.

It was dark when Boy's father came home. Immediately, Boy knew that something was wrong.

'It's Cyfarthfa. The villagers had a meeting. They say he's got to go.'

'Go?' asked Boy. 'Go where?'

His father shrugged. 'Anywhere except here.'

Boy felt his stomach growing huge, tumbling like an autumn leaf. 'But what if he doesn't want to go?'

'Then they'll make him.'

64

Boy was on his feet now, shouting. 'But they can't, Dad, they can't – – – – –.'

His father put an arm around Boy's shoulder. 'I'm sorry, son, but he's dangerous. It was only luck that Dai Jones wasn't killed today.'

'Cyfarthfa didn't try to hurt him, Dad, honest. He saved him and his stupid boat from the rocks.'

Boy's father shook his head. 'It doesn't matter. They've made their decision. Cyfarthfa's got to go – for the sake of the village.'

Boy felt tears pricking at his eyes. He pushed his father's arm away and ran for the door. He raced up the steep hill towards the dragon's cave. Behind him he saw yellow lights flickering. The villagers were coming.

Finally Boy reached the dragon's cave, the opening a deeper black against a wall of solid darkness. It was cold up here and Boy was suddenly afraid.

'Cyfarthfa?'

From inside the cave came a low rumble.

'Yes? Who is it?'

The voice was deep and loud but it was not unfriendly.

'It's me, Boy, from the village.'

'I know you,' said the voice. 'I've seen you watching me.'

And suddenly the dragon was there, in front of him. Cyfarthfa's huge eyes shone and Boy could see his chest rising and falling with the rhythm of his breathing. Clearly the dragon was as nervous as he was.

'Cyfarthfa, you've got to go.'

'Go?' said the puzzled dragon. 'Go where?'

'Anywhere. The villagers are coming. They think you tried to kill Dai Jones. They're coming to drive you away.'

'They wouldn't hurt me,' Cyfarthfa said, staring at the village that had been his home for a thousand years.

'Look,' called Boy, pointing down the hill, 'can you see those lights? It's the men from the village, coming for you.'

The dragon snorted and bared his teeth. 'Then I'll fight them,' he declared.

Boy shook his head. 'You can't beat them, there are too many of them. You've got to get away.'

65

Cyfarthfa stared at the lights, knowing Boy was right. 'But where can I go?' he asked.

'The Preseli Mountains,' said Boy. 'The rocks will hide you. With your colour nobody will ever pick you out. You'll be camouflaged and safe.'

The dragon nodded. 'Very well. I have no wish to hurt the villagers. They've let me live here for a long time. I'll go.'

The lights were close now, a few hundred metres below them. Boy could hear their shouts, Dai Jones's cruel bark among them.

'We're coming for you, dragon,' he called.

'Please go,' pleaded Boy. 'Quickly.'

Cyfarthfa smiled at him. 'Come with me. So you'll see where I am.'

Boy shook his head. How could he? Then he heard the shouts of the villagers again and knew that he would do anything to get the dragon to safety.

'All right,' he declared. 'I'll come.'

He climbed onto the dragon's back. To his surprise Cyfarthfa's skin was soft and warm, like a new blanket or a piece of rare silk.

'Hold tight,' called Cyfarthfa.

There was a rush of air and, instinctively, Boy closed his eyes. When he opened them they were high up in the night sky with the lights of the village far below. He clung to Cyfarthfa's neck.

'Watch,' breathed the dragon.

He swept down towards the advancing villagers, scattering them like skittles down the hillside. Boy saw Dai Jones tumbling over the rocks. The man sat up and shook his fist as the dragon shot away towards the Preseli Mountains.

It took them some time but eventually Cyfarthfa found what he was looking for – a lonely cluster of rocks high up on the mountainside.

'This,' he said, 'will do nicely.' He glanced at Boy. 'You will come and see me sometimes, won't you?'

'Of course,' said Boy. 'I'll come every week.'

Cyfarthfa shook his head, sadly.

'You'll come until you grow up. Then you will forget.'

'No, Cyfarthfa,' Boy cried, burying his head in the dragon's chest. 'I'll

66

never forget. I'll always come, always.'

'Well,' said Cyfarthfa, 'perhaps you will. And perhaps I might even go back to the village one day.'

But he never did go back. Once Boy and his father told the villagers the truth about *Pelican* they began to miss the dragon and wish he was still there. But gradually, like all grown-ups, they lost interest in magical things like dragons. Soon, most of them had forgotten Cyfarthfa even existed.

Dai Jones never forgot. To the end of his days he was a lonely, haunted man. The villagers grew to hate him, though they had forgotten why. Sometimes in the night Dai would wake up sweating and afraid, regretting the wrong he had done.

Boy did not forget either. Every week he cycled into the Preseli Mountains to see his friend. Even after he grew up and moved away from Pembrokeshire he always came back several times a year to visit Cyfarthfa. On one visit he painted a picture of the great dragon with his talons tangled in the fishing net. Cyfarthfa posed happily for the portrait.

The painting hangs on Boy's wall, a reminder – not that he ever needs one – of Cyfarthfa's courage and strength, and a record of the sad day when the village lost its dragon.

When Merlin's Back

Catherine Fisher

Listen. I'll tell you my story.
　My father had a boat; when I was ten
　he'd sometimes let me row it round the bay.
　That afternoon looked sunny when I started,
　sky blue and clear as a gull's eye,
　but I'd hardly reached the headland when a gale
　raged round Stack Rock.
　　　　　　　　　Waves pounded;
shoulders of water shrugged me up and down,
slopped, slapped, soaked, sneezed,
swallowed me up and spat me out,
numb oars skidding from my fingers.
Shaken and flung and rattled I huddled
knee-deep in spray. The storm had wings
that roared and creaked. I said prayers. I cried.
I curled up. I thought I was dead.

When I opened my eyes the hush was a shock.
Hours had passed. My lashes were stuck,
hands clenched white. But I was afloat.
The boat was in a cave, deep underground.
Somewhere ahead in the tunnel redness glowed;
a rumble, like a great belly's hunger
plopped drops from roof to sea. I breathed
sulphur, and the sting of salt.
Oarless, the boat slipped down the steady current.

68

It grew warmer. I stopped shivering,
thought I'd been swallowed alive
by a beast of stone, a cavewhale, a serpent's
vast throat. All the walls were charred;
fissured and scarred as if some great bulk
had been dragged by.
                    Another rumble.
                                   Heat.

So hot now steam drifted from the surface,
and leaning over I could see my face,
scared, rippling in shallows.

The boat beached with a bump.

I fell out. Too stiff to stand I rubbed
knees and ankles. My clothing clung to me;
shingle slithered, sent me staggering.
Fishbones in heaps as high as my head
stank and clattered.
                    I kept very quiet.

Round a corner the rumble came again
a snore, a purr, a throb, red as heat.
Tugging my feet, silent as I could
I slid and slithered round the nub of rock.

At first I thought the enormous cave was empty.
Its walls were scaled and slabbed; crust of weed
grew in crevices, ridged stone overlapped.
Somewhere though that throb vibrated
in my teeth and nerves, my fingers' ends.
I twisted them tight, said quietly, 'Hello?'

An eye opened.

Unlidded, in the side of the cave. A soft
leathery slither, a creak. Frozen, I stared.
The eye stared back, as big as I was,
slotted black pupil, yellow and gold. An eyebrow arched.
It looked me over.
                    I swallowed.
                                   Backed.
The whole rock slab uprooted then and turned,

69

pebbles and gravel rattling from its chinks
and I saw it was a head, an enormous narrow head
with long snout and nostrils steaming
like fumeroles. It hissed. And suddenly
I realized the whole cave was a creature
wrapped around me, hunched and fossilized
and ancient as the rocks, weed-grown, vaster
than I could see, shadow-vast, its nearest folded wing
pustuled, the rib through the blackened crusted leather
knobbly and thick as my arm.
                              Steam rose.
And a voice, delicate as silk, sweet as treacle.
              What are you?
                                    My answer

was a stammer. 'A boy. Sir. Just a boy.'

Indeed. I haven't seen a boy up close for years.
Another golden eye creaked wide. *Are you a knight?*
'No.'
        A saint. Like Derfel?
                              'No sir, no. No saint.
A little devil sometimes, my mam says.'
A hiss. Like sarcasm, like a laugh. Behind me
a scaly limb came round and two great claws
picked me up and turned me, put me down,
breathless. *I see. Then you must be a thief,*
come here to steal. I can't have that.
Nor will I enter into riddle games, or roll
to show you my one vulnerable spot.
I'm too old and cunning.
If I may advise you, boy, say prayers.
I'm afraid I must devour you.

It must have been his tongue. It slid from darkness
that opened in the rock; I saw teeth in there, each one
iron hard, serrated. Muscles rippled under
the buckled hide. I said 'Sir. I promise you.
I wouldn't know what to steal.'

His laughter was a rumble and a quake.
Lumps of stone tumbled; dust rose.

Little boys, he said, *don't use their eyes.*

Wiping mine dry, I stared round, indignant,
determined to find out what he meant.
Maybe it was the beam of sunlight that slid in
from somewhere high, that made me see.
Maybe the dragon's scorn had cleared my eyes.

It wasn't sand. It was thick and yellow and
there were heaps of it, piles and stacks and
mountains of it. Not sand, no. Too beautiful,
too bright. Ankle deep in gold I saw its light
ripple on the rock walls, on the plates
that were the armour of the beast.
There were jewels too, ruby and carbuncle,
topaz and emerald and diamond and pearls,
spilling from boxes crushed under his body:
and rusted metal swords and crowns,
crusted with barnacles. Cups and shields
and boxes of moidores tinkled as he snorted,
bracelets and rings, china things,
pieces of TV sets, computer keyboards
and remote controls. He flicked one at me
with his iron nail. *Modern treasure.*
No use to me. Once when ships went down
the sea shone with bullion. Now men
value circuits. A dragon loves beauty.
His long mouth like a crevice in the rock
cracked to a crooked smile.
How are things out there? Is Merlin back?
I stared. 'Merlin the wizard?
He died long ago, and so did Derfel
and Arthur. All those men from books.'

Books! The eyes slotted with wrath.
They were real. And Merlin won't be dead.
Holed up in some magic hill no doubt.
He shifted. *I haven't been out*
for a few centuries. Perhaps I should
spread my wings. If I stay sleeping here
too long my fires will slumber;
I'll turn to stone for good, crumbling

72

like the surface of the rocks. Those
planes though, I don't like their roar
coming over at night. A battle with them
might be chancy. Need to train for that.
Now boy. Close your eyes. I will be quick.

I stepped back. His mouth was wide,
a cavern, fishy-stinking, sulphurous.
Weed hung from his teeth. 'Look,'
I said, 'I've got a better idea.
Let me go. I won't say a word.
No one would believe me if did.
I'm far too small and gristly to chew
and besides, they'd come to look for me,
Dad, and my uncles.'
                    Are they knights?
he asked, sleepily.
      'Sort of. Lifeboat men.'
         The dragon yawned. *Dear me.*
              I must apologize. Conversation
                 is all very well but I need rest.
                    Let's get this over.
                          His claw closed round me.
                 Each nail was an iron bar. Squeezed
                 in his grip I gasped 'One last request.'
                 How tiresome. What?
                          'To sing.'
                 Sing?

'A hymn. It's what they do
in movies when the big ship's going down.'
Again he yawned. *How very dull,* he said.
Do hurry.
My voice was quavery and weak,
it sent drips splatting from the rocks.
I chose For Those in Peril on the Sea;
they sang it in the church up on the cliff;
I knew each verse. Softly and quietly I sang,
making it sad, a lullaby, hushing
the ripples in the cave, soothing
with sound the warm dark place.

73

The great eye watching me blinked once,
and blinked again, and then closed up,
slowly, like a sunset over the hill.
And joining in with me the dragon's snore
rose and grumbled far under the ground;
small particles of rock detached and rolled
into the heaps of gold.

Still singing, humming,
keeping my voice low, I climbed
the iron ladder of his nails, over and down
ridged scales, walking backwards through
hills of gold, watching his eye's faint
sliver of amber. Snoring,
the great beast stirred and dreamed,
a circle of mythology all round me,
red and deep and fissured, old as Wales.
deadly and wise. Breathless, tense
with dread my fingers found the boat;
I scrambled in, desperate for an oar.
From the hoard a rusted sword stuck out;
I used it, dipping the blade into the sea;
the boat prised from the bank, floated, turned.
Far ahead the cavemouth opened.

Don't ask how I got back. They picked me up
hours later; I remember Dad leaning over
saying, 'Wake up, son. Wake up.
Where have you been?'
I never told them, though. I'd made a promise
and kept it. And the sword, when I groped for it
had gone to small red fragments in the boat.

For years, I tried to find that cave again.
I never could. Sometimes now on moonlit nights
I stare out at the headland, think I see
the outline of the beast curled under there
guarding his treasure, hot streams his veins,
the rocks and stones his body.

Maybe when Merlin's back, he'll slither out
scatter ships with his tail, roar, stretch, yawn.
Win his battle with the planes.

74

Bladderwrack and Driftwood

Malachy Doyle

'Steady, now, Bladderwrack. Steady, now. Let's put it here, behind this stick.'

'Fat lot of good that'll do, big brother,' said the smaller dragon, scowling at the tiny piece of seaweed they'd just spent fifteen minutes carrying up the beach. 'The tide'll come in and wash the whole thing away, just like it does every day, and we'll have to start again tomorrow.'

'Well, what else can we do, little brother? It's a dragon's job, as I keep telling you – building sea defences, piling up whatever we can find to try and protect humans from the mighty ocean.'

'Fair enough, Driftwood. Fair enough, in the days of our forefathers, when we could shift tons of sand into the right place just by blowing at it. Fair enough, when we could pull great tree trunks out of the forest and pile them deep into the sand to slow down the waves. Fair enough, when we could blow fire at the sun, to bring on the summer and dry up the rain. But now?'

'Now what?' Driftwood was fed up with his younger brother's moaning. What was the point of going on and on about the state of the world? Why not just accept your lot, and get on with it?

'Now that we're nothing more than glorified crabs!' cried Bladderwrack, stamping on the sand with his spiky little foot. 'Now that all we can shift are pebbles and shells, seaweed and crisp packets! Now that all our fiery breath is fit for is to light the coals of people's barbecues! Now that it's not just the

75

pounding of the waves we've got to try and stop, anyway, but the never-ending rise in sea levels. Can't you see it's hopeless? Completely hopeless!'

'Oh, for goodness' sake, little brother,' said Driftwood. 'Flutter off to Aberystwyth and do a degree in Ecology, if you're so obsessed! Just leave me here to get on with my job.'

So Bladderwrack opened out his tiny corrugated wings and fluttered off into the sand dunes, while Driftwood spied an oily feather and added it to his pile.

'What can I do?' the little dragon asked himself, buzzing over the caravans. 'How can I protect these silly people from the ocean and themselves?'

Year by year he'd watched the tide, slicing away at the dunes. Another few winters, and the water would breach them. The sea would come rushing in and swallow up the caravan site, gobble up the golf course and begin its steady progress through the village. A hundred years and there'd be no one left. The water would have destroyed the harbour, drowned the houses, risen to the top of St. Peter's, and the Bells of Aberdyfi would ring no more.

'Who cares?' he thought, giving way to despair. 'Who cares about all these dim-witted humans, anyway? It's their own stupid fault, messing about with the world. Filling it with motor cars and aeroplanes. Stuffing it full of factories, belching out their foul-smelling fumes. Mucking around with everything till the ice caps are melting, the gentle warming waters of the Gulf Stream are in danger of disappearing off into the Atlantic Ocean, and the ozone layer, way above the clouds, is punctured worse than a beach ball.'

And the way they treat the dragons! The only creatures on earth who ever understood what it was all about, were hunted and hated by man. Feared by the very animal they made it their mission to protect. Driven from the land, to the high mountains and the western seaboard. Pursued even then, so they had to make themselves smaller and smaller until they were almost invisible. Skulking among rocks, sheltering in the sand dunes, feeding off the scraps left behind by holidaymakers and fishermen. What sort of a life was that? What sort of pride can you have in yourself, when all that's left is the blueness of your skin, the sharpness of your claws, and your red-hot chilli-pepper breath?

76

'Who are you?' said the child, leaning down over him. 'What are you saying?'

And Bladderwrack realised that he'd been mumbling and moaning and drawing attention to himself, as he pondered on the troubles of the land.

Too late, he thought, to hide. Too late to find a handy rabbit-hole in the dunes and startle a few bunnies with a well-aimed ball of fire.

'I'm a dragon,' he said, bowing his crested head to the child. 'A dragon, at your service.'

'You're a bit small for a dragon, aren't you?' asked the child, peering down at him.

'You may have read about us in storybooks, young man.' Bladderwrack looked him in the eye. 'But I'm just the size I should be. I'm smaller than my brother, but I'm bigger than my sister.'

'So am I,' said the child, nodding seriously. And from that moment they were friends. 'What's your name?'

'Bladderwrack,' said Bladderwrack.

'Like the seaweed?' asked the boy.

'Like the seaweed,' agreed the dragon, pleased to find that he was talking to a human who at least knew something about something.

'My name's Dorian,' said the boy. 'And I'm nine. How old are you?'

'Eighty-seven,' replied the dragon.

'Eighty-seven!' cried the boy. 'Eighty-seven years old!'

'Yes,' said the dragon, nodding. 'That's only young in the life of a dragon.'

And he felt an urgent need, right there and then, to share his troubles with this thoughtful little boy. He started to talk about the pebbles and the seaweed, the Gulf Stream and the ozone layer.

'May I take you to school, Mister Bladderwrack?' asked Dorian, after a while.

'Why, is that where you're going?'

'Yes. And if I don't hurry up, I'll be late.'

So Dorian pulled out his sandwich box, gobbled up his packed lunch (he gave the pepper salami to the dragon, who thought it was wonderful), and popped Bladderwrack inside.

The dragon blew a few holes in the lid, so he'd be able to breathe, and off they went.

78

'I can smell plastic,' said Miss Evangelina Davies, sniffing the air as they filed into the classroom. 'Melting plastic.'

But no one owned up to anything.

'What's this, Dorian?' asked the teacher, a few minutes later, looking at the scorch marks on the front of his homework book.

'I don't know, Miss,' said Dorian, who didn't know.

'It looks like a burn mark to me.' Miss Davies raised her eyebrows. 'Have you been playing with fire?'

'No, miss. I haven't, miss,' answered Dorian, suddenly realising what must have happened and kicking his bag well in under the table.

'That smell of plastic, Dorian…' Miss Davies crinkled up her pretty little nose. 'I'm sure it's coming from round here, somewhere.'

'No, miss. I don't think so, miss.'

But Miss Evangelina Davies wasn't one to be put off the scent. She leant in, through the forest of legs, and pulled out Dorian's bag. And, as she did so, a streak of flame shot up from inside and scorched her moustache (for she had a tiny thin line of hair on her upper lip which you could only see if you looked really closely. Or, at least, she used to have).

'Ouch!' she yelled, hurling the bag to the floor in surprise. The lid came flying off the sandwich box and Bladderwrack, terrified, hopped out and raced towards the open door.

'My dragon!' cried Dorian.

'Your dragon?' exclaimed the flabbergasted teacher, as wide-eyed children ran hither and thither.

'It's all right,' Dorian reassured them. 'He won't hurt you.' And he rushed from the room, after the frightened dragon.

'Bladderwrack! Bladderwrack, where are you?' he cried, and found him at last, cowering under the caretaker's rucksack, in the broom cupboard.

'She's OK, really, is Miss Davies,' said the boy, picking him up and smoothing down his troubled hackles. 'I wanted to show you to her, anyway.'

So Dorian carried the dragon back into the classroom and asked the teacher's permission to bring him up to the front of the class and introduce him to everyone.

79

'This is Bladderwrack,' he said, once the children had calmed down enough to hear him. 'He's a very small, very friendly, dragon.'

'No, I'm not,' said the dragon, and everyone gasped, even more amazed to hear him speak.

'Sorry, no. He's not very small,' said Dorian. 'He's smaller than his brother but he's bigger than his sister. Like me.'

'And me,' added Miss Evangelina Davies, licking her top lip to cool it down.

'Hello, everyone,' said the dragon, forcing a smile.

'Hello,' answered the class, edging forward to have a good look at him. But keeping well out of Bladderwrack's firing range, just in case he turned vicious.

'I'm a dragon,' said the dragon, and as he looked at all the eager faces, peering down at him, he knew what he had to do. 'I need your help,' he said.

And he proceeded to tell them about the ice caps and the ozone layer, the Gulf Stream and the disappearing fish stocks. And even though they'd heard most of it before – for Miss Evangelina Davies was an excellent teacher, who'd always known that there was a lot more to the job of educating children than just reading, writing and ticking a few boxes – somehow it seemed to the class much more real and more urgent, hearing it from the mouth of a very tiny dragon, there on the desk in front of them. Especially when they heard about his brother, Driftwood, down on the beach, trying to save the world with a few oily feathers and a pile of sparkling shells.

'So will you help us?' the dragon asked them. 'Because we can't do it all by ourselves.'

And they all said yes, and vowed to do whatever they could to spread the word across the world – that the future belonged to children, that the dragons were their friends, and that there was hope for everyone yet, if people would only learn how to live for tomorrow, and not just today.